Unquiet Wind

Jennie Clarke

Paula,

Stay in the
light

J

1/47

Canadian Cataloguing in Publication Data
Clarke, Jennie
Unquiet Wind
Poems.
ISBN: 97809817773913

1.Poetry - Collection 2. Poetry and Prose 3. Women and
Culture
I. Title
PN 1042.P4 2016
811.6 CLA

Published by: EndaStampa Press
Toronto, Ontario

Cover Illustrator: Spencer Afonso
www.spencerafonso.com

Dedication

To my father, Peter

Jennie is a beacon of light who sees the chaos around her and moves it

~ J.L

~ Prologue

This collection is a poetic journey through the human condition. In these words, you will hear vivid portrayals of the human encounters with despair, grief, longing, lust, hope, love and divinity - a powerful journey through the levels of human consciousness. Let me present a viewpoint, which may signpost the divinity present underneath the words in this collection of art.

Time and time again in human history, it is out of the depth of the agony of despair that people have awakened up to the divinity, the depth of being that was there all along. They have discovered that which makes the knowing and experience of life possible moment by moment. They have realized that they are not their emotions, their life histories, their memories, their beliefs, their bodies, but they are the one awareness in which these things take place.

This awareness is what all "others" are too underneath the diverse appearances. In this awareness, we move and have our being. The awareness of "everyone else" is as real as "mine" "You" and "me" can be regarded as different points of perception in one consciousness, one life, one being. We are all interconnected, all animated by one breathe of life. This consciousness, this ultimate reality, is love without conditions. Totally affirming, totally accepting, and totally embracing.

The human mind can scarcely grasp the reality of divinity loving us not in spite of who we are, but exactly AS we are. We, humanity, are loved infinitely, perfectly, totally **WITH** all our pain, trauma and apparent mistakes. We are invited to quit judging ourselves, quit judging others, and accept this love - a love that loves us just as much whether we accept the invitation or not.

The more we recognize the unconditional love of divinity for ourselves, the more we can love others unconditionally. This is the basis of compassion. This poetry shines light into those aspects of ourselves we might rather avoid; it exposes the repressed nightmares we would prefer to forge. The more we bring the light of acceptance of all aspects of our psyche including the darker emotions — the more we can transcend them. Often we try to repress those parts of ourselves that we think are unlovable, yet nothing is unlovable in Reality.

Everything, which is illuminated by the light becomes part of the light. The human condition is part of Life, we are part of Life, and Life is the game of Divine Love, even if that love sometimes seems very deeply disguised. Very often, we find in life, that with hindsight difficult circumstances can be seen to have mysteriously worked out for good, that even hitting rock bottom was a necessary step in our evolution. Love was the highest intention behind all that we experienced whatever the intentions of the individual actors in the Play of Life.

Underneath all the happenings and drama of life, so vividly captured in this collection, everlasting unconditional love is our true nature. This is the mystic secret of the ages; this is the good news.

Love, peace, and blessings,

Joseph Cash
Author of **"This is The Dream"** and **"Beyond Identity"**

~ The Poet's Curse

What rests in the hands of the reader once the poem has been read? As a writer, I would like to think that communication has been made, thought has been provoked, feeling has immersed, and wisdom has been gained. Poetry is not about summarizing the poet, but understanding the images. The first thing to note is that poetry is not an essay, report, short story, or epic. The greatest mistake one can make as a reader is assuming poetry is unequivocal. A poet will take several different images and mix them together with contradictory statements. This is done because poetry is an art form, and what you read and what a poet says can and may have separate meanings. Multiple meanings or expressions of an object, an image, a thought, or some form of wisdom is what poetry is about, at least for me. Poetry offers no plot, character, or data. If it did, there would be no uniqueness to it. Despite all this lack of "meaning", poetry means what it needs to mean for the individual.

Approaching a poem needs to be done with a clear mind: there should be little focus on the writer, although I understand that this can be difficult. When you begin to read, ask yourself several questions: what is it about? What images stand out? Is it about dilemma, love, happiness, despair, or tragedy? Most reader's first reaction or question is, is it biographical? This seems to be a huge focus that poets do not care for. The poet is irrelevant: the question really should be what does the poem mean, say, do for you? What can you learn from or take away from it? Who can you read it with or to, who will appreciate it? Not, why did the poet write this.

There is no secret code to a poet's soul: keep in mind that poets indeed suffer a curse of language, mirrors and truth. There is no convenience of meaning that is right in front of you as you read. I do not purport to be anything I am not. Poetry is emotionally intelligent but not informative. There is no need to pursue the poet when reading the poetry. Line for line, broken down, some with meaning, some without, some will swamp you into to nothingness, some will grip at your heart. But whatever it does, it does for you as the reader and not for you as your connection to the poet.

Poets answer the questions of human action and reactions. They are not afraid of death or love. A poet can imply but this does not mean they have lived it. Au contraire, probing for meaning will never get you closer to the heart of the Poet.

When I am asked why I wrote a certain piece, I feel as if my artwork that I so carefully unpeeled in layers from my heart has been stomped upon. I do not purport to be witty, intelligent or meaning-driven. I struggle to play with words. Fundamentally my poems are maps of people I encounter every day. Some are parallel to my own life, and some are others asking me to be their voice. I take no direction from poets, I simply am.   As poetry should be — not necessarily "mean" but "be". Poetry is about force. It works when it is felt. It functions when it is visualized. It offers counsel and consoles those in pain. Poetry is healing and rapture along with loss and gloom. At least to me, that is what poetry is.

Damn. How much damage can you do with a pen?

Eminem

*I want to stay as close to the edge as
I can without going over.
Out on the edge you see all kinds of things
you can't see from the center.*

Kurt Vonnegut

Memories to Illusions to Sorrow

Change is the end result of all true learning.

~ **Leo Buscaglia**

~ I

have the courage to stand alone
and take on your demons
in order to end this suffering
               see cause
I have the faith in faithless
but trust is where the heart lies
and well see
I have the courage
to fight the conversation
in the fire   and
in my wake state
I know I was revealing truths to you
               see
I can take the stabs
because I know damn well
they aren't about me
                    and see
I have the love
the love that says
you don't have to speak
because your hands hold me
                    and see
I have the diction to not
kill you with venom but
kindness
what you never showed me
and see if you stop taking my words
and turning them to save me
from me
you'd
               see
it's ain't me that needs the saving

~ Where are your eyes

Where are your eyes
That you get caught up in her being
I live in a broken heart
Across the Styrofoam cup
Placed on the kitchen counter
And all I ask is that you love me
Unconditionally seeing me for me and not letting my spirit bleed
Where are your eyes
Stretched around her voluptuous breasts
And you are so turned on by her smile
And you can't help to feel her love
she welcomes this new realm of life encircling her jaws and
tightening its grip bleeding at the gums that enclose her teeth
Where are your eyes
When you see her shape
You meet, for the first time,
And you move throughout her,
ever so slowly
she starts to cry tearing her blouse open
witnessing the wound gushing of worrisome nights
Where are your eyes
when you question her demons, her past
and shout out your cries
as you tear away your anger
for the troubles in your life
and all she wanted was your hand in hers, in time

~ Aidan

I will not contribute
to your loss
it only harbours
my own

I will not be selfish
to your tears
yet mine taste of Aidan
do yours?

I will not be resentful
to this god
for he does not decide
my right

I will tell you I miss my own
son this day
because I could not
give him life

I will set this grief free someday
when his wings are fully formed
and tell him that it was because of him
that his little brother was born.

I will see the shadows of his footprints
in the sidewalks next to mine
and hold his hand ever so tightly
as this death was so unkind.

~ Elizabeth

Elizabeth was your birth name

Angelica,
I gave to you
when you gave birth to me.

Your eyes so fond and lovely,
who took you to the stars?
Angelica my darling, come home
you are so very far.

Pastures green and mountains high
Angelica went too soon when she died.
Who would have known it was to be
that I would love her desperately.

Past the river and down the banks
through the town and off the planks,
beat the drums and play the horns,
for the body is gone, thus we mourn

Graced with beauty
oceans high
I missed to tell my longing's cry
when trees and branches swipe me by
I feel your spirit
and begin to cry.

~ *Azrael*

A stiff awkwardness
months of fighting the flight that
came down and took hold of his heart
Azrael takes to pew
in darkness 24/7
his boundless wings cover the book of life
with his notes of death
erasing the lives of those he takes
as he smiles greedily, looking behind
and adds to the column to the left of death my papa's name

I grip the locket of dead zoned losses
in conversation I speak to the most High
Azrael please your hands human as my own
please bring him back to me   there is more to speak

but no consolation comes my way
and he adds more grief
blank empty altars, he bends on knees   praying
and sadness swallows up my flesh
Oh delicata carne
oh soul please speak to me

A morning of rushed wind
maneuvering my car to arrive hours later
a foyer of deafening quiet
backwards to my mother's tired arms
a paleness of secrets kept

she, frozen stone, speech
less
Stiff cold awkwardness
Azrael proud of himself
with stomps on skull my brain dead   from grieving

How pathetic we are as human beings
philosophical engagement of falsehood
meditating for strength
praying for peace
not understanding how truly weak we are
when it comes to death
just stop the bullshit   and speak

It seems death has come to prove this point to me
bragging about the constant visits
draining the longevity of his stay through me
moving strangely into and out of dreams
he brings friends now with him
they stand at my bedroom door
staring at me
There's a feeling that never quite
leaves you when death
comes knocking
a feeling you've been swept
away from your own busyness
and thrown into a whirlwind of
stop   wait
I can't breathe
the world you knew

abruptly falls at the seams
of your life
and now   time?
death offers no rehearsal
there is no practicing moods or tones
and suddenly
unexpectedly
you're on your knees begging   why?
Could he have stayed a preference?
so we could have him back in our lives?

Paramount loss of a game over
and now the lullaby no longer sounds sweet
row row row your boat
papa
gently thrown the fog of paradise
merrily merrily merrily merrily
life sure wasn't so sweet
but you kept telling us to live the dream

smashing memories
fill the void
so I am told
you're gone
a mortal coil
slumbering in a coffin now
with a draped banner of words and I?

Prefer to grieve alone
to die alone
I would prefer to die alone

~ Veils

there is a veil between life and death
and grief stricken is ever present
loss is inevitable
but this heart just cannot let go
i told him i loved him in May
again my words of this came in July
and the response was a calm
"i know"

the fitted passion
that wedged its way around
every risk i took in life
the furious independence
stirring from his ever present dialogue
straight shooting to my limbs
all memories now drift into isolation

he left all he loved behind
to go home
he no longer speaks
tho he comes now in dreams
and i am ripped apart from his eyes
there are stories undisguised
as my mind shrinks
my heart just can't let go
i wait for the magnificent vision
of fog in the morning
something tells me he will
be my guide

and not this feeling he is lost at sea
where my sorrow joins the outer banks
wrapping itself in a blanket of waves
i want the thoughts of death to leave me
to change this negative portrait
to the image of brilliant colours
that i miss so
and for him to take my heart toward the other side
so i can sit for just one more time

Peter, hard as a rock. Nervous yet calm and poised. Unfamiliar with privilege. Young, uneducated, apprentice carpenter, black suit fits loosely against his white crumpled tie. The tie crosses the sole dark blue button. His curly blonde hair tightly dressed on his head. The scent of his cologne, cheap but sweet. His skin dripping with olive oil. Patent leather black pointed tip shoes with rockabilly heels for the nights of escape. The shy charm revealed in his half embarrassed but please-look-at-me smile. Ray-Bans shelter his excitement. His hands invisibly tied with now dormant fears of failure. The darkness of each lens engrosses my wonder of who he really was. Peter, a Marconi cigarette sits loosely against his bottom lip. One of the few photographs he has of his childhood. None prior to the age of 18 were taken. Memories become so important and legacy through stories are all that are left. The story becomes more magical and unrealistic as the generations speak it. He is romanticized now. There is hope for some truth. He is everything to me, and nothing. He is the light. The heart shaped glass of my future, my internal pain and my external body. The potency of his hands will lead him to work and to love. A maroon suitcase, next to his leg, waiting to be placed against a seat on the train leaving Bolzano to Reggio where love awaits.

*~ **H**ail Holy Mother of God*

He is a clumsy old man
His wife still irons his work shirts
He retired a decade ago
She dusts off the black beaded rosary
she takes from his shirt pocket
every morning
monotone movements
He gets dressed for her mercy
Sits at the desk in the musky basement
Books on accounting recounting meaningless figures
He stays there for hours
A convicted nomad
She is suffering from a mad fever
There is vicious argument in her head
daily
If steps should change
this confirms she is old
her figure is meaningless
He struggles with the vicious wife's mind
The comfort in old for him is good
supper time
sound of car keys bounce against the foyer table top
Let's pretend the work day is done
He plays on words recounting the accounting
She brings him spice.less animal corpse and greens
She waits
he eats
she strangles him from behind
Holy Mercy Mother of God

~ Conversations

You will never see me in the sunshine
how striking you are to me
how I love the sensation of
your demonstrative hands
my lips of temptress wine
the sound of your velvety clouded voice

illusions

I am worried
you will never know me
because we are two doomed ships
who have crossed lines
so many times
you move with haste
passing my vessel

memories

We are stuck in a space
where the windows are painted shut
and the smell of gasoline
has become normal and fragrant-like
we lapse in disguise
we move in marked territory
and live with average

sorrow

Gifts

Love consists of this: Two solitudes, that meet, protect and greet each other.

~ **Rainer Maria Rilke**

tonight I lean my face against your cheek
we, poets, are more intimate in words
diction to the lover's **pocketbook**
a bulk of landscaped muse penning a paper
aching for someone to read them

You rest on my mind
ready for your translation of love
there have been moments my aura goes blind
that powerful sensation of you
between my thighs
vibrating

primavera

you, speechless, yet, pounding love

I am lost in your eyes

rumours chasing heads away from each other
delicious desires of you in my slumber
how does one recall the night spent in sex with poet
leaning bodies and striving thrusts

I do not want to be a phrase
in your pocketbook
of poetry
I want to be your poem

I watched you sitting there
at the table with the checkerboard
mounted in the stone
your fingers beating against it
looking down at your pad
reading and rereading the things you
needed to tell her
your curly blonde hair, long, untidy and dirty
clothes stained and mouth dry
and I wondered who she was to put you,
lovely you,
in this state
not once did you look up
noticing only the words floating on the page
as the water streamed up closer
gentle waves teasing you to have a glance their way

I wanted to walk over to you but
who was I, like the ocean
unnoticed

you stopped beating,
writing now, flipping back, scratching your head
and wiping your sweaty brow
I watched and waited, hoping you would move away
from what ailed you, the pad, the page, a love
but you never moved

~ Milk

the box terrace home stinging for life
the smoky skies fill it
the northern side of who I am
and I watch from my window
never drawing the net curtains

I see him coming from Sunday to Thursday
5 am on the clock on my kitchen wall
he looks haggard, annoyed,
quiet
I want to love him
undress before him

the clatter of time moves forward
twisting us into forms of impatience
words have lived latent within us
I want to be his heart's desire
but the bottle is all he holds now

streets of cobblestones
the webs we lace to distance our feet
the pubs filled with young roses
he enters them on Friday night
I long for him to enter me

~ *Vinegar*

It is an unfortunate tale within the community.
They have suggested the death of her son has made her crazy now.
The other child sits in a prison cell all in the name of "love"
If you approach the front door there is an aroma of vinegar.
She uses it to clean her body
In the heat, if she ventures outside,
you can actually see it dripping from her nipples before you smell it
She is so tormented by this lose she thinks that vinegar will disguise
her sadness

Her eyes are daunting and filled with question marks
Mothers gather around her to encirclement her, to pray with her
For a brief moment she takes them with arms extended and
embracing
Until she realizes they have not lost as she has
They turn from mothers to murders in her mind
And the room where the love takes place become more
Tortured desperate crying for help for feeling so alone

He drove too fast over the valley of the suburban stars
it had been a year since they clasped lips and minds
he was still green when it came to understanding pure love
at this point she was only showing him a "good time"
As he approached he heard a familiar laughter from the distance
then again, he heard but two
as he reached the bend to where they made love
he saw his brother and his muse

18

~ *Parking*

The rough times should have been over by now
So the cards told me about a week ago
Yet I still find myself sitting alone at Sheffield Park
Watching the couple with their newborn and enjoying themselves

I wonder where the yellow teeth I see in my mirror came from
Sure I brushed away all the blood every morning
And my hair is matted around the back
I guess I did not do a good job in this regard either

I am a quite sad about the last 60 years of my life
There were things I was supposed to do and take care of and didn't
I forgot to look after my knee and am having trouble walking now
The vegans keep telling me to come in but I am not very trusting

My heart is heavier than my car and even heavier are my shoulders
The pressure on my blood meter is larger than the weight of my
head
If tears wash the eyes, I need windshield blades made of steel
Focusing on the road ahead is futile with every changing of the
clock

There is no point in carrying forward
My mind resides closed of memories of the past
No book or prophet can possibly alter my moods anymore
Whatever is done has now become another lost skin cell
nothing more

~ *Gates*

I want to know you

the you before you left

that tow-path we walked together

those blue trousers and that hat

fit tailor style

I want to remember you fussing

to open the cast ironed gate

looking around mortified with embarrassment

blushing

but you got it opened

the gate

leading

to

I want to see you again without fallen wings

before the plane

passed into the wrong direction

before you took the last breath

           and entered the unquiet sky

Perceptions

People only see what they are prepared to see.

~ **Ralph Waldo Emerson**

~ *The Delivery*

The delivery was present

Dubliners packed the streets to watch them arrive

Mammy going on baby 11

Would she really bring another one home this time?

Crowds of drunkards hard at work

Stealing dole money off their wives

Whilst the sun dimmed over the road

To the house of many brothers, mine

The main gate where the car was parked

My ugly faced father accompanied mushy heat

Mammy's grave overtones, half-eyed misery

What fools in rolling hills we must have appeared like?

Father only wanted things we simply were not

removed and calm

Father

"a shag shouldn't always lead to this messy lot!"

Pause

Mother

"Indeed my dear, but we are Catholic"

~ *In-difference*

The toll is high against Laura
pressure of clots not flowing right
people wanting a piece of what is not theirs to have
inflictions of already scarred zones

She feels the indifference for those that talk
about things that need not be their business
but life is dreadful on their end
thus her world shows a better dialogue

and gossip IS the devil's radio
surrounded by miscreant faces
"Did you know she so and so and so?"
Did you even ask me if I cared?

Desensitize mind when the preachers enter
the judges of this life are not one of kind
tune the radio to the left for damnation
or push the off button on their mouths
one time

~ *The Gossipers*

It was rather revolting
That devil's radio – self-made, proclaimed,
retention and named
They talked about her
"ere comes the ol mended whore"
GOSIPPERS
"She fucks em dark blokes ye know"
RIGHTEOUS
"a brood lot to feed after them nights of shagging"
UNAMUSED
Talk trickles over tea
Swollen hags wondering where their husbands are whilst watching
another virgin's hole leave for the night.
"She's looking for the meaty hand to pay for her cunt"
SHOCKING
"Oh Mary must we use such words!"
BLAME
"It's true you know, I heard from a lady at the grocers"
At least they were faithful
SMIRK
At least they stayed in and paddled their babies with a wooden
spoon to get them to bed early
Early enough to put on their self-made radio for the devils' talk
Why, what else was there?
An eruption when their husbands came home
PISSED
At least talking about the fur-collared whore made them feel
important

INSIGHTFUL
generations of ideal chat
baby upon baby tuned in
everything seemed morbid as the kettle boiled
the bag was put in the pot
the cubes passed around
at least the ginger snaps weren't stale
Margaret always kept the front window clear and clean
the folded chairs unsnapped
to position their arses in line again
at least the virgin never disappointed – never once- to give these
women a bit of purpose
PERCEPTION
and just as their terrace stood symmetrical to the next
as did their bums
uniformly positioned chairs numbered
their husbands departing labour and
arriving home, had their tea, slept briefly then
gathered their hat and coat
LEFT
there was always a little peck for assurance
"I shan't be long love"
whilst down the dreadful road he trotted
 over the mud puddles in the rain

RADIO - TALK
the virgin always left shortly thereafter
in the same direction
but this was never given meaning
"what? – no – silly woman, she didn't go that way?"
Silently they sat, elbow to elbow
MORTIFIED
drowning into the faint light
Half one all gone
Half two all gone
Emptiness on the streets
HOME
Henry returned singing,
"Let me call you sweetheart I'm in"
"Shhhhhhh"
Margaret charged the stairs to help him in
up to bed
dragging his shoulders
heaving him up
It got cold during the night
Margaret reached for the window to shut it
as she reached to close the curtains
she looked down
there walked the whore
"I'm in love with youuuuuuu"
SILENT

So, the night fell on the village of twitching curtains

~ Amused

Perplexity amuses this ghost with the false faces we see.
Rich maniacal tramps that sit in waiting for the world to come to
their feet.

Judgment haunts their past as
they so beg condemnation onto me.
Weak words made to criticize my muse
feeds from corpses that bleed.

Gains in numbers and fake plastic hearts,
of posing to be righteous, yet wrapped in their own lark.
Designing a life of mainstream gypsies with tattooed skin and
penniless wastebaskets of saving worthless pride
now trashed in bins.

Gray, gloomy and cold against the cellars of eyes
Pretending to be gentle with Muse is **not** wise.
Reinventing the pages and recreating the name
Yet soiling the friendships so anxiously gained.

Older and lonely, uglier than spoiled wine,
a stench of false praying and the pot-smoking smiles.
Crouching down on twisted knees, a beseeching tone,
will never compare, pathetically, as you are left to moan.

~ My looking glass self

it's on the tube
where Ava sees herself
through the old dear
with rags on and her fancy English hat

it's through the street
where she witnesses her mind's eye
the mother grabbing onto her child
while juggling bags of clothes from the thrift shop

it's through the park
where Ava see lovers cuddling
and feels alone again
left wondering where she went wrong
now searching for her cigarettes

it's through the vagabond
where she envisions her father
and pleads with him to stop
with the bottle, begging
for forgiveness for being alive

it's through *the looking glass*
where one will witness the stars
and pray for light to come
with better memories
and chapters filled with delight

~ I Cut into You

I cut into your hands
you who popped me
with your lucid tongue

I cut into your hands
you who wrote God's words
on the ends of my fingertips

I cut into your hands
you who broke my back
with gravity chasing pulls

those lamps, that light, the streets, the voices
the women who walk the night
from working for the men
carrying knives to protect themselves
from the hands that cut
following the brakes of the cars
that echo and honk for them
to come and cut into their hands

~ My Drug Lord

the laughter through my ghetto gate
the heroin drops on my silver plate
the leftovers of foes gone astray
and I am nothing without my fame

plastic people all around
the chemical smiles from their frowns
the drugs that keep us bent in shape
and I am everything for just one day

mediocre ain't where I am at
hustling the streets for my crack
the world my oyster in thick hands
and I gain freedom in a zipper bag

you keep me steady in this artificial space
you are my friend without a face
the dreadlock lover that I chase
and I am dancing through your lace

the light that never seems to fade
my magic mushroom where I lay
through the fields of opium gaze
you drag my arms of needle track haze

*~ **B**leak to brighter notes of love*

Oh Heavenly night
I sing at your feet
and tears that flow
are whispering *please*

Do not take this love
from my precious heart
O Heavenly Father
I want what is not
Thy wings I have clipped
with sorrow removed
and fly I will go
in the arms of this muse

To be by his side
gracious o night
sing to the skies
of bliss o delight

O heavenly, O August
by moonlight be still
O heavenly, O December
by sunshine be still

~ *Rubber Band*

She bellows in whispers; her mouth broadens like a rubber band
and nothing is heard around these senior walls; it only surrounds
her
all day
  all too long
   all in the end
The anguish a heavy weight on her heart
remembering the places that eased her
Does no one see her face exploding?
Who can say what she feels if we are not living her life?

There is no excuse for her damnation
but she feels it every day; a dementia of loneliness
she tries to smile, to carry on and trust in herself.
She sits alone in this crowded room rocking
slowly against the wooden floor, mad trickeries enter her soul
Mold holds the walls up;
As black as the blanket of night
No food to nourish her bones
Bruises on her hips that no longer sway
In the right directions
Rubber band rocking chair; hard life moves at a quicker pace.

~ Sacred Prostitute

a different bed

new pair of shimmering eyes

smell of ancient stench

a fucked up toilet

my glass is always unfilled

in the morning

no more which

colour makeup I have

"John" has disappeared

the least he could have said was

'need a ride?'

I stumble off the bed

made of coiled rubber sheets

now wet from last night's

forced lovemaking

the bathroom sink

looks the same as the last one

odious white bowls

no marks, no stories,

are comforted in my imagination

my shoes have been chewed at

that damned invisible dog

the window is mushroomed

it's hard to see the cars

passing to go to work

my day is done

love is an intersection

it never lasts an eternity

it comes with a price

each night

along with

an aching burn

~ Emotions

Intense emotions avoiding all just to be alone
Competing with the ego, tis as she is known
The moments of discomfort rip through your bones
Facing yourself is necessary in order to grow
Urgent messages race straight to your soul
Aligning all perceptions about who I am
and what you aren't
Paradoxes are mirrors of blessings in disguise
If my words take over there will be no bias
I serve no purpose in this world completely
Worthy not are my actions without drawing in deeply
Affirming confidence and self assurance takes times
Renewing my faithful interventions for all things Divine

You can take me
make me
shake me
to whatever you please
control me
and
than scold me
but
never seize
to remember that I am human too,
and
I bleed
I am tired of the shit you believe
so if you fuck with me
the walls will close in
and you will
feel
empty
again

~ Back

she wanted those things back

the things from the days when

his cotton t-shirt soaked in scented oils

off his skin that draped around her ribs

one raw fibre unprocessed

she wanted those days where he was her

poetry and she was his lavender bath

watching the candles lit, dancing gently

to the healing music around them

and after this the tantric fest of sexual

orgasmic blows, of ecstasy drug-infused nights

exploding through her veins and lashing out

an uncontrollable laughter releasing, hours later,

deafening tears of guilt and pain

she wanted the love that lived in her home to be

freed of the perceptions of curvier spines that tried to

rest on her back and blame her for love that did not

belong to them and she is now constantly reminded of

the knotting of serpents sliding around and her terror of

chopping their heads off

and what karmic inheritance this might bring,

so she holds back

but they keep coming and barking at her door,

angry that they did not get a chance inside,

the mind games of others who just did not understand

their life.

She wants those things
that took away her dignity
and spread pink liquid
through her chest cavity
of jealousy and ruin

to heave backwards into their manic hearts and

feed themselves with what she never hungered for.

She wants the life of sanity, of sleep, of contentment

but

it sits by her side pleading for her

to surrender

so that it might

be a tidal wave of acuity that she needs

as there is no awareness between indifference

without her acceptance that

all she wants is near

Always be ready to speak your mind
and the base man will avoid you.
~ William Blake

~ Echoing

They have all left me
I, now the last coffee bean
a reverberating tin sound
the roar of spinning alone
I tried to dig this hole from under me
Wanting, simply, to come home
to taste the aroma of warmth
becoming weightless within my fear
and bound never more
watering the dry plants arching my feet

closure is contradiction when words are tasteless

excelling in my fastened space
accepting no one is near
in this wasteful crowd
where I shrink to the core of insignificance
angry at the chaos
monologues written the night before
by faceless religious undertones

my tongue hollow with truth
grabbing at the lies that are disguised
lose yourself I say
lose your identity

Physical

Now he has departed from this strange world a little ahead of me.

~Albert Einstein

There are moments when all the questions we want
answered in times of distress
are not present.

There are puzzle pieces laying against our feet that we
cannot reach immediately
and when we do they do not seem to fit.

There are visions of everlasting physical life,
that when it is taken so abruptly we are left hanging like an
unfinished painting that seems dull now.

Aren't paintings supposed to be beautiful?

When we approach all this there remains only one answer.
That is, that nothing truly matters but Love.

It is here,
it is in this energy
that is Love
that life and death are unseen
and
all that is
and
is of profound consequence
is Love
as Love is Infinite and with love
one requires nothing more.

Dedicated to Colin and Joseph

~ Luca

The day my brother died
I could hear the family breathing downstairs.
My upper bedroom carried vent sounds
of tears from my mother's heart.

Papa talked about the jar shut tight.
Canada placed him in it when he died.
There was nothing like this in the old country.
Mother wept with tormented eyes.

He was born still from waking.
The deaf tones of my mother's laborious pains;
petrified that she would lose him.
She passed out before he pushed through.

Today the walls close in when we enter the house.
A smell of bleach everywhere,
as if my mother longs to tidy
this reminiscence of coming home

bare

~ Corridors

I am the corridor William took to see his first born child, and on me he stood weeping as he looked through the glass and worried about what kind of father he would be.

I am the corridor leading to Spencer's first day in school, where he was afraid to leave his mother's hand although she constantly reminded him that she would return, but Spencer did not believe her.

I am the corridor of the hospital where Glenda was rushed after being hit by a truck on her way to work, and Craig ran along me with the nurses shouting out to her that he would ring her family to tell them she was ok.

I am the corridor of Tom's first performance night where he walked up and down me chain-smoking, because he was afraid to be seen as a failure in front of his first audience.

I am the corridor in the church hall where everyone gathered the day Angie's father died, and she couldn't help herself but to hand out tissues to the mourners, as she had no tears left inside.

I am the corridor Alex ran through the night he left his wife, up in the flat without warning that he was going to leave again, but only this time he decided to empty her purse and take her keys.

~ Jenny

The rain barely spits against my creeping jenny in the garden
I so wish she would not tease and give jenny the chance to grow
The wind slows down the dance from jenny
and swirls are quiet still
I'm hoping the raindrops will come and rest upon my jenny

~

the earliest gardens my grandfather used to dig away at
remind me now how delicate our gardens can be
these gardens too, of love and friendship
now a soft, fragile hand to rest upon me

~

I so wish the rain would fall and sit against my jenny
reminding us to enjoy the moments we have and breathe
to feel the company of crisp yellow flowers
that jenny springs in June to deliver to me

~ December

<u>1:13 a.m.</u>
The dead of night is a comforting place
A warm car turning over the crushing of snow on tires
He remembers his mother dying
holding now his wife's hand as she breathes in
For him it is all unfamiliar
He depends on her to lead the way
There is a quietness on the floor
Nurses whispering plans for the weekend
Giggling from lack of sleep and old coffee
He looks distant and so afraid
Her waves of strength and fatigue
keep him centered

<u>1:45 a.m.</u>

Sounds of eye brewing piercing howls
Turning to whimpers of pain
Wheeling her into the freshly blue painted room
He never let's go of her hand
African Canadian doctor
Her saving grace
Strong women assisting with birth
foaming white lights
a violently loud push
tears stream down his face
A son

~ Rocks

For Virginia Woolf

The night drew in, unforgiving and long
I sat in waiting to hear your accustomed movements
  Lined up on the sheets that we lay in
  were the rocks I collected from the roads near our home

I heard my brother chanting alone
like a songbird with bright spirits
  His love song so sadly unheard and rehearsed
  for the woman that strained his soul

What little time I had left here for you
and you were out of sight
  I dressed with your trousers held up by your belt
  meticulously placed each rock within

The ferocious beast in me soon to rest
Forlorn and broken at best
  Down the swamp with Angel's wings,
  Hail the thunder, at last my soul sings

Worthy not to heaven's gate
lay me down on the cold water slate
  Tempted hell on my lover's fate
  the wind that found me came too late

Anima

Forgiveness is not an occasional act; it is a constant attitude

~ **Martin Luther King Jr.**

~ The Pack

In my dreams, I shall not meet you
at the station by the spring
for when I wake it is all for nothing
that the mirror reflection is not mine

Years ago when I had you
I hurried away from your reach
now with gesturing voice you call me
yet this love affair can never be

For with tired hands you held out
Slowly, twice I died for thee
and for what was all this muse
more in vain to not let us be

You who came upon me bathing
all temptress lust and pinning tales
me of heart and abandoned sounds
vowed this love would never fail

in my dreams you shall not visit
to carry out what was not meant to be
I rest my life within your love
and ask you to forgive me

You are nevermore within my womb
    But as the unquiet wind crawls toward my spine
I feel you
  The unborn child they call you
this label is so undefined
    Resting over my heart is your little hand in mine
On this day and every day, you
  Sweet child
    By loving Divine

I watch you on that swing
  Kicking your heels so high
     there is a laughter that meets the winds
It is yours and mine

you are gone
but not forgotten
in your space
remains my heart
lying naked on the tiled floor
waiting patiently for you
to return to me
to start it again
a *sanctified* moment blurred in my mind
the vigorous way about you
in your fierce manner
you left me standing
naked and vulnerable
once sanctified and full of grace
now I am weak
from your anger
the only place I feel holy is on the floor
I don't know the reason why
I made you angry,
this time,
but you are gone,
in your space
remains my heart
lying naked on the damp floor
I wait
for you
to come again

memory

~ *And from Afar I Awaken*

the urgency of the morning never fits in my plans
it would take away my sleep-walking and staring mind
summoning for stillness around the room I shared with him
watching him slowly breathing in his dreams

I picked him up from the tavern close to Becky's house
She lived miles away from me
I picked him literally off the kerb and hailed the taxi for home

there was a moment when I pulled the sheets off him
my handsome man with his curved broken knees
bent out like a crushed wave in a unquiet wind
I wondered, dangerously so, what I loved about his body
the driven caressing of waves through my veins
he touched me while he talked
and lit my cigarette
yet
he wasn't like the younger ones
honest, Intelligent and unimpressed with daily dribbles
there was an book of mature scent to his staleness

and whilst the months persisted
I watched my life go by his windowpane
the joy of our meet died
he was no longer a train stop to Euston Station
Now
he was the dead seagull on the prom in Blackpool

there was little resistance in him
thus more the reason to make him mine

Ho
preso
una
ferita
profonda
scuro
e
l'ho
portato
con
me
fino
morì

Il
perdono
perso
nel
tempo,
nello
spazio
della
morte,
in
questo,
la mia vita

~ Drowning

Binding my tail
soft scales overlapping
pry thee amidst my eyes

Surrounded in an irksome light
around the chute of the waterfall
seize me not from gushing
into fastened arms

If only for love,
spirits suffer in vain

You quiver around me
sinking your teeth right through me
See into me
If not for the outer layer
I would bring you my blood
in the holiest cup
knotted and refined
of Celtic spirit
and lurking faces

Spill on my arms
Outstretched and opened
Surge through my being
seek the hollow deliverance

now

perdonami

~ A lonely Summer

dad developed a massive swelling
on his heart
the doctor said it could not be removed

in six months
operations, radiation and cancer
deceased

he died a day later
our last visit was a discussion
about going fishing in the summer

~ Soul

You must remember me when time
is misery and can't help me erase the pain of life
You must take me to the rooms of frameless memories
where the monumental silence is kept

Forlorn traps of what could have been
where life blossomed on those cool fall nights
and evergreen leaves lay tingling my bare feet
yet sounds of tunneling tears that I still weep

You must remember to smash the pavement
of where I briefly met his eyes
You must take me to the bedrooms of tireless nights
where only our shadows remain now

only our shadows remain now

Significant

The great art of life is sensation, to feel that we exist, even in pain.

~ **Lord Byron**

~ The Womb

I recall
the night when my brother made way
for me around my mother's womb.

It was as if he had decided
he did not want to be in this world
so he threw me closer toward
the placenta of her grief.

She stopped feeding me days later.
She sensed the deal my brother
cast with God and this made her
coarse with me.

Born

I recall only one sound.
my right ear not being able
to hear anything
as my left ear had overextended itself.

It was my father crying from the other room.

Her boundless abandoning stopped
the music from entering.
The more I talked,
the quieter I became.

~ *Unrequited Love*

I threw all my dreams into his eyes and yet every breath I reached at the ends off my voice box still sounded unclear. His vision forever darkened by the stars of my hopes that pierced with persistence in the wrong direction. I slashed up and down, as side to side never drew the correct amount of blood leaving his mouth dry with blame. For all the times I tried to follow my dreams, he insisted to sit against the jealous moon and watch me die.

Of course I had every intention to love him, but the moments of urgency stabbing my heart to just.let.it.go outweighed the polished love making scenes I recorded

I craved

I archived

in my manic wired head now it had to be done, so that I could carry on feeling his presence lost and found in the hallows of the wind because despite my grip to keep his chest against mine with every bit of intention to love him.

In this garden state of hope
where the fiend reflects her childhood
Ora contemplates all that her mother should have been.
In her refuge of silence,
she waits patiently for absolute love.

This is the least she could have given to Ora.
All that she is, now, futile rejection and gutted loathing.
This, she will not force upon her womb.

A photograph of father holding her close to his chest,
whilst sisters stand to either side of his strength.
She is wrapped,
firmly,
from the warm sun touching her face.
Tighter from his skin daring to touch this Love,
he will become her disease,
Yet, in the end, it will be she who will rise.

Creeping in low income with fears
of going blind and still waiting,
father comes to mind and Ora begins to cry.

He holds the glass cracked cup fueled with a tank of booze
His hands are the hammers
that beat down mother's spirit.
She, the child that stands in the middle
to save them from each other.
Yet, now, as this child, she, alone, gets by.

the front porch

Made of concrete cell-like
man filled prison echoes
built from father's thick hands
where he drank at night
every night

the front porch

Chairs from the kitchen table
wrapped in patterns of the old country
brown mixed with yellow and orange dead flowers
we were not the envy of the neighbours
only mocked by them

the front porch

The philosophical sofa
where stories unfolded about
father's sadness
and the red wine
tainted my thoughts
remnants of alcohol wet my hair

the front porch

Spelling textbook wide open
studying my words for the next day
while the tears from my father's eyes
dripped from pain onto the page
as I shouted out words in foreign tongues to please him

the front porch

Archways "times" four
brown brick distinguished the Italians
from the Protestants
mother was never seen sitting with us

the front porch

Around the corner from the garage
my father took the kitchen chair
walked with stride steps
determined
focused

the garage
the invisible tight-rope
the last conversation
hopeless

~ Joseph

My grandfather always wore his work trousers
He was humble
I was only a little girl
I know he worked the field from dawn to dusk
and walked eight miles to reach home
The same suitcase style of woven donkey hairs
carried his meals three a day
The shovel of steel made a groove alongside
his back where it lay during the journey home
His hat was not fancy like the men in the shops
It was of soft cotton to keep the sweat off
I remember him holding my hand in his
not understanding the voices of passersby
The musk, the soil and the rain carried
themselves on his skin especially his arms.
The sight of the potatoes in the marketplace
digging for them was his life

I wonder now that he is gone
why his tapestry had been undefined
He was a religious man, always seeking truth,
and so stubborn yet so shy
From birth to death, I lived with him
I longed to take his smile
To place it on my sons faces to
show that love was worth the while
His Vespa rests against the garage now and his
hat still hangs in its place
His shovel is rusty, old and retired
but his memory is my carrying place

~ *Ricordando*

Energy
off the coast of remembrance
that one marked memory of time
when I was worth everything
I will tell you now my skin has chilled, dry, hard
the indicator of this deathly present life
what do you know about the European women?
what do you think you know?
I had so much faith in the father
more faith in the church and marriage
until I left home
here the Book of Laws slammed into my passageways
here where choices were made
even though I convinced myself they were MINE!
mirrored the "more fool me"
robbed of the threshold gardens of a wondrous life
shocked from the rockets - minus - stars in the skies
my generation was not my mother's
although I tried
God. Damn(ed). You.
I tried
I am the identity of the deceased daughters
- none of them survived
and their voices
silent sleeping silent

~ Another Man

unable to explain the grind and sperm between her teeth
she recaps false reminiscences of last night lived
forming a vision of something horrible
where darkness is a part of the scenery
he does not buy it
the slammed door between her ears
he's gone

time now is all that stays with her
free falling through the hollow room where he left her
the sound of shattering muse crossing over the bed
her mind makes up why she cannot remember
fate spelling out letters on her bones
a naked figure

there is no story left to tell now
He does not come back to listen
She wants to believe it was the right decision
after all is life not already planned?

the choice of sleeping with another man

Lovers don't finally meet somewhere;
they're in each other all along.
~ Rumi

~ *Recalling Rosita*

I remember when she was about 95

lived off the corner brick hut

in the southernmost part of Italy

about 15 miles from our home

on the mountain

sometimes she would get a ride

into the village to come see us

even, at 95

she always carried her crochet handbag

by her side

plump and delicately voluptuous

she had strawberry lips

and seven daughters

she shouted when she cooked or prayed

made love in h

if you mentioned Tomas to her

her eyes arched forward and

a black wave passed in front of her

They place a tattoo upon your heart

not for us to see

black lines chasing white streets

leading to rooms, fermented and unknown

your father, your uncle, your brothers stared

hoping they would be the next one in

to see the damage never repaired

Your mother took the money

your sister paid the deeds

your aunties combed your hair

pretty Alla, if you please?

and all you ever wanted

was a bit of tenderness

Alla, holy prostitute,

boys and men, who knew you best

your tattoo spoke of swords

against your darkened skin

to pierce

into your chest it lies

Alla,

please don't die?

you waited in a room

spilling cum from the walls

praying for the lull within

a wooden narrow hall

a bed

spread her legs for lust
unwillingly every time
but did it in fear
for fear of the knives
she lay her head at night
looked over to the moon
no tears came easily to her
her destiny, her doom

she died

They say the way to a woman's heart is flowers,

especially roses,

apparently I am supposed to get excited when

I see chocolate.

In fact, I am told that

chocolate and roses will "win me".

This makes me feel quite branded – like a cow.

Imagine his surprise when he sat next to me

on my porch that evening.

Children, gone, grown up now and left.

I find myself alone but it isn't painful

I can still read his mind, about me,

after all years of begging to be free.

He came from around the back of my homestead

thought he was being clever

In one hand the roses, a smell of them

done gave me a headache

In the other, chocolate, I can't eat chocolate anymore.

Not that I ever did but nowadays with few teeth left

chocolate is not my first choice.

He is sweet, always had been sweet, but he isn't what wins

my heart.

that there be poetry

The deluge of fruitful diction, the bold nouns, verbs

and adjectives that take us beyond

our granite minds to similes.

that there be poetry

The silence as I sit in my room

the attachments of love, and loathing all on one page

that there be poetry

Where dreams are acceptable and you can be

whatever style, whatever size, whatever name

whatever relentless wish you want to be.

There is no prize for love with chocolate and roses
but there is a price for me
Words spoken
Words written
Poetry

~ Smeared Dress

Your offending eyes undressed me
your angry smile mistreated me
tonight was filled with regret
and I didn't even know you yet.

Up against the wall I slammed
you were going to be the man
that took my fortress within my tree
a wrath seethed inside of me.

Your hands were larger than my might
that bled upon the darkened night
your knees broke open my sacred grace
into my hole, my vessel place.

You filled it up with such disgrace
tonight I knew what was my place
smeared dress against the glass
selection of poison or grass
I chose the first to die quick
you forced the second
a massive stick.

Against my lips, I took it in
and gasped what was left within.
A smeared dress of Burberry scent
pit of hell, where I went

Innocent

Do you hate people?
I don't hate them; I just feel better when they are not around.

~ **Charles Bukowski**

*~ **On Being Ignored***

Pampering words
when you need me
are never enough

You continue to represent
what you are not

I speak only in a true tongue
you are bad for my health

The abortion of us is not over
Thick syringe filled with toxic blood

Spews out from my mouth to your ears
longing in the form of

Being ignored

Act it out in the skull space of the mind
Apathy for your mourning fills my rhyme

The coma you are in is done via a mask,
injecting your stillness like heroin destroys the task

~ *Dawn*

still and black as the ended night
and it makes no difference to
those on trains
For every moment
and every Nazi
commands standing two in a row
mother and child
now act as strangers

listen to the bombs in the distance
an accustomed sound
barbed wire fences are home
fingertips to freedom vanish
And *man's search for meaning*?
Despite the loud comments of death, looming
the gas chambers, the water, the view
the bird in the cage
the tea in the cup
the stripes on pant legs
the piles of false teeth
the pregnant young
the hold to the present
the fear of the lines
the dirt on sore feet

Forgive them
Forgive them, for they only know fear

~ Cancer

My mother's pain started
with a breast ache; a visit with that which is in "charge"
brushing off her words as a "whining wife"
"what do you think you have cancer?"
a gesture of ignorance
a bill of tablets to fill
homeward
continuing routines
My mother's pain is worse than ever
with two breast aches
strokes of trouble
a check-up requested
by ignorance of in "charge"
cancer care finds her name
on the folder
she rises and sinks into my arms
my mother's spirit swims
through me like a wave of fear
I am a slow-moving dead man
I weight the same size as her
but I am not dying physically
walking up the stairs to her room
my mother will die in her bed
no waiting rooms for her
screaming hallways of dying souls
I am 19, I am reluctant to speak
I don't want to say goodbye
I am disbelief, impatience
the next visit her trouble finding words
swimming in and out of coma
don't die

~ *Old Age*

Speak, even if one no longer listens
to the infinite traps of life
swaying with brittle bones
in order to position herself with ease on the sofa
dislocate what was already useless
take that last tablet no matter how it kills you
short sighted by the narrow opinions
love flew away years ago
life now leaves from being still
it has been too long overdone
should she feel happy with little words
away from the hustling of voices
the dance was never dull
murmurs now memories fading
he used to touch her
there
some time she remembers him
that side of brain is empty from aging
left in its place are scars of birthing everyone who stood near
the sceneries they covered together
fled fast from her mind
humming dormant now
longing
and
weeping from aging

~ Volare

Parasites filled her belly
and the doctor suggests she stop smoking

she thinks it's the Greek salad from yesterday's bistro date
maybe she won't stay at the Stratford Hotel tonight
her body seems to shut down from the heat in the room
the snow outside dresses the weeds

she could have sworn she felt
several bed bugs on her neck

tomorrow is minutes away from waking

Maybe she'll call Roach in the morning
they could drive to the Rideau Canal together,
that is,
if he isn't too busy

it's been a long year
she reserves no judgments
the order of things persists as
God's Will

the pillars of blood now turn
and the writing is never lost as they told her

Poverty, created without thought,
yet awareness throws blades and spreads light

~ *Unwanted*

Did you know you were unwanted

your philosophy of nothingness

always untrue

and as mysterious as a cat

Did you see the gift I gave you

or were the signs censored

recharging relationships

never did come that easy

Did you think I would be so foolish

To fall for your tragic story-again

That the woman in me

Would be beckoned by hopeless romance

Did you count those days with me

The days where you stole my thoughts

sorting them like trophies

collecting my vagina in your dusty box

Did you forget the faithlessness you drove

in one direction toward my eyes

how foolish, how foolish am I now?

Ask the elements to protect you,

oh no

love is so unkind

You and your magical wand

misleading me and my life

I was waiting for you

pacing for you to bring back my age

youthful love with hands up my shirt

but you went even higher and ate my words

Did you not notice the medal of courage

resting on my mantle near to your sword

you know the one you left under your pillow -

surprise.

~ *Parallel to You*

Annie's veins run parallel
Insanity bathes in the lining of her bedroom walls
And she retreats to the shell where she is safe
yet to others she stands the Iron Maiden that never falls

It was just yesterday when Annie was proud
of whom she was
If only she knew about all the mistakes,
she was to make
Her voice box now closed
She has killed herself several times today

Blinded and strangled by the dark dog demons
They never seem to sleep or rest
The dialogue that should be sweet
Drills a hole of loathing, making for a mess

Her mantra fastens her in constant form
For hope to ride and steal her away
No more hallucinations of grandeur
Denial keeps your voice astray

~ Steps

heavy steps
turning purple
cannot take the pressure
of my tiny soles
my rubber band mouth
heavy breasts
twisted nipples
inverted by the mouths
of babies suckling
my rubber band mouth stretches
heavy hands
tapping lightly
against the writing pads
of my rage
my rubber band mouth stretches to scream
heavy heart
tracing memories
about the life
spent
my rubber band mouth stretches to scream - sonno
now going cold
gone cold
tainted dreams now gone cold
delicate beings recklessly sold

i am the old woman i have been told
that sits unrested
and gone cold

~ Fatal Nights

Weave the wound and wrap the blood

sterile needles that puncture this love

gauge the gush spreading through your hand

pick up the wound for it falls like sand

seize the weapon you thrash on my chest

crawl before this rage-filled mess

carry the cup you shared with me

banishing desire that shall never be

damn the day I found you lonely

pity the fool I would become

taste my yearning that screams your name

and suck me dry with *muse* that shames

murder my will this hollow eve

stroke my wit and let me be!

~ Murder Me

Greed

that eats daily at my stomach

a deadly twisted form of apathy for you

spanking my intellect

caressing my moods

craving for someone that is never true

speak works of a damned poet

always transpires but never really exists

revulsion swims on the stream of disgust for you

like a spider caught in a black web

you form too many confusing questions in my mind

bitterness and hatred are what you feed it

gluttony so powerful

it could kill instantly on impact

I only hunger for the mortal truth

that love does not live here in this house

freaking, frantically waiting for

no reply from you

this is all you give to me

a tenderness of poison

corrosion of minds

the search is now ending

the spider is caught up in this web

that her only choice is understandable

she knows it all too well

yet this too has come too soon

strangulation

a very small neck

won't take a moment of your

precious time

You'll return being what you are
they stand around her
fence her in

the smell of manure lingers
throughout the fields of farmland
rain sent damp morning dew

they laugh as she shakes
from cold, from fear, from despair

the first one moves forward, slowly stuttering in his tracks
he is gruesome, fat slipping out of untidy trousers
smothering his lips on her
groping his way

punching and patting her down
like a boxer

she is knocked out from disgust

he bends, barely looking up

only momentarily

seeking the approval of his mates

the laughter, the chanting begins

he enters the virgin hole
bangs away at her so hard that

the others stand like trophies proud of his accomplishment
he rises, victorious

wipes his brow and throws his semen on her
she lies dormant as the next places his piece in her
on and on this goes

screams of violence within her mind tearing at the laces
she has used and reused to sew her soul

the last one
breaks the circle, he is angry and ignorant of the others

looking down at the virgin he is brought to tears
with one arm he lifts her and holds her close to his heart

can she hear the laughter around her
no one knows

~ Routines

Last night you came back
sturdy shoulders and swollen belly
from the night out with your mates

I hate when this happens but
it does twice a week
and all too well you are going to speak

There are times when I sit on the floor
hidden behind the front door of our house
and pray you do not return home

Maybe the fog will whisk you up
so I don't have to bear the burden of your
vile plastic teeth shouting at me, again

How rushed my life is when you are away
remembering what makes you angry is exhausting
"don't leave the dishes in the sink"

My routine is ritual, habitual, compared to yours
the nights out consist of hanging your clothes
hoping Julie doesn't see the bruise from next door

There it is, the dreaded key sound through the hole
"Where are you! Get down here this minute!"

I am, down here,
you kicked me again coming in,
someday, I hope you miss

~ Hannah

Hannah's womb remained dormant
Untaken of children
no man could fill it
She was never eternal
Only came as a guest
Into the man's house
She had taken her life
To many rooms over the years

her forest remains dark, stained and soiled

Safety clips force folds of her skin shut tight
yet one part remains unfastened
Overextending her world
The clock ticks biologically inside
Setting off missiles from her uterus
Tubes filled with blood and semen
Trapped, swimming and smashing
Into one another

~ Frigid Bones

Frigid mantling skin off my brittle bones
with dried palms and eyes wet from frost
my layers do not keep me warm
the heavy air brings the current home.

Entering with remoteness in my heart
wiping the ice columns from my brow
you sit pale eyed with your cup of tea
placing the screws into my feet.

There is no shelter from the deafening light
the sun rests now on the other side
where the universe is greener with delight
and my green moon feels wrongs from right.

Colours of opium twisted through red
on the bed where I lay your gruesome head
from the twilight gale that storms our room
where you told me you wanted me much too soon.
The hours were ours to keep in the night
while rain beckoned the earth's flight.

I carry my feelings through shades of grey

and watch from the window where you lay.

The hours of dusk emerge as you open your eyes

bones fragile from your face hung portraits this night

and the scent of you I no longer desired

set flames in your soul of a cursed fire.

Frigid feelings sit next to my hands

crippling my fingers taped to rubber bands

seizing my words that remain cold from your cries

it was for your muse that this worship has died

coating me gorgeous with treasures and wine

to succumb to an object of sexual twine

i yarn you up to set myself free

You gave me no comfort when you came inside me

~ Your Wooden Floor

Scratching at the bedpost

claws extended

I creep down with poise

abandoning your selfish erection

hoping you do not wake up

I am leaving you

with a massive spider web on your face

I hope you aren't too upset

I warned you

not to shout out my name

it will be harder to forget me now

No handshake when I finally

meet you at the gate

I know you will not be pleased

to see me, this time,

considering the mess I have left

around your eyes.

No uncomfortable embrace,

which means I do not have to wear a sweater

to avoid it

I detest your sour look

tired of you soaring through your body

wandering aimlessly in that one cell that

holds together your thoughts

I reach the ground

where your life sits

collecting dust and jagged hairs

shaved from days gone by.

I can hear your teeth grinding

your flesh moves in your bed

your greasy forehead drips with panic

turn over

please

~ Trapped

My tires slash your body when you cross.

I find you lying against the curve of the road

filled with debris and stones.

It is hard to get myself up, my knees tremble,

petrified, I move toward you.

Along the side of the car,

residues, remnants of your private parts.

The air filled with flesh and mortality.

I want to close my eyes and make you vanish but

that is not going to happen yet.

Head decapitated from your body.

Extensions of what you were lay to my left and my right.

Funny, I am not afraid of you this time.

All the moments of abashing are out of sight.

I, once, arranged myself next to you every night

praying that the tablets I had just taken

would dissolve as quickly as

your hand reached for me.

I do not want you anymore

deceiving myself that I did

because I was afraid to be alone.

Now

I am trapped in the crossfire

of your sins.

You were desperate to control my every inspiration,

nervous to please and appease,

to calm my movements.

Yet my words danced around your doubts

typing against your forehead with

that assaulting pressure.

I step closer to make sure I got you.

Forward with anticipation and relief, you are leaving me.

My movements curiously look down.

It is the only part of you I recognize.

Mangled beautifully
swimming in a velvet bath
rests your soul.

I got you

trapped before your hand reached my cunt

Her rooms

A woman knows the face of the man she loves like a sailor knows the open sea.

~ Honoré de Balzac

~ *Old Photographs*

The old photographs lay on the desk waiting to be filed,
like the memories stored in the vault of my mind.
They have rested in this place for years now,
accumulating over time like cobwebs.
Cobwebs that lead me from the desk
to the room we once shared together.
Together where you told me that I was every
new day and long luminous night.
Nights that swept past us as you embraced me
restlessly laying within our bed.
Bed of solitude gathers near the old photographs now,
like the dust forming against your specs.
Specs of visions that drive home what we once were,
myriad laughter and joy encircles your lips.
Lips melt watering turned to manic rage,
when I found you with her, the anger I had.
Had it not been for this,
the old photographs would have remained new.
New patterns of leaves form on my branches now,
of the misfit I have become.
Becoming whispers in conversation,
and a scorned face in old photographs of new.

~ Canopy

What pleasantries we have shared
underneath this magnificent canopy
filled with light
thoughts of liveliness and ease
as the stars flickered in the night
And to think I used to see the light of day
from this dark and fragile sky
and all I dreamed of was you,
sparkling with your elegant eyes
an empty canopy is all that is left
the day that our thoughts died.

It was December when you set it up
I prepared myself for the fall
yet sometimes it shocked with its warmth and
it surprised me with its calls.
At night, I would sit inside it
the closest link to you
and I would feel all around it
rough around the edges, yet so brand new
There were moments when I thought
it could never drop too low
and then it would shock me again
perhaps telling me there was no more warmth

In the spring, our canopy closed for good
and, yes, of course, I cried
but it told me that there was love between us
despite whatever died.

~ Crucified

when you smooth over your words,
in your eyes I still can see the fierceness of your loneliness
like marbles falling on concrete
shattering the opening of who you are not

it's loud and bitter
your expressions are
of one being raped
they speak in a tongue so unordinary
intense and dishonest
but this is what drives them to exist
and all their complicated lies
surround those delusions

I watch your face
I see you have crucified yourself
weeping eyes and a somber stare
you are a survivor of the lust and hatred
but I still see the slash around your neck
that is something you cannot hide
but under the force that consumes you, you must turn green
like the leaves on the trees in springtime
you cannot escape this, this your truth, your beauty

you go home each night
the walls that surround your perfect space
are thick enough to warm your spirit
for the next day
and when you return, they remain the same.

~ Surrender

on a night like this one

even when manic looks good

you rush my branches

chasing me with your bend-skinned eyes

and despite this disease I feel

the hunt is easy as I give in too quick

my roots start to show

what little water I have left to feed from

buds do not grow here with care

I see nothing but the layers of smoke

compressing my thoughts to stay

in a place of agony with *no surrender*

requirements to conform with guilt cards

that lay next to your contagious games

my strength is knowing what they say

the weakness of unfounded self-esteem

the day urges me to rise

manic screaming towards the disgust

and drowning out the risk to win

injury and neglect dive in

a figure fat, low, stacked with paranoia

immobile and bond with need

the branches wilt and decent

a lump of coal

is left of me

~ *Haunted*

I am haunted by the space I live in
By the experiences that you are not a part of
The breakers of emotional void left me of human experience
The unknown words to come
and the inconsolable tick that sits in my ear tube
breathing
whispering
crying ever so softly

> I am haunted by the temporary happiness
> stale smiles on my doorstep
> loose handshakes and hugs
> the carved holes within my lips
> with lacking goodbyes, I failed to send

> > I am haunted by the intertwined ache of physical
> > illness and mental attacks
> > gripping my heart and squeezing your name
> > with silent sobbing
> > stories in tears
> > dried cheeks
> > of Kleenex boxes.

~ Human Beings

For Charles Bukowski

A minor difficulty called
work
we get up and it is a fucking rat race
to get there only to be shafted by the
miserable twat we call the Boss
A major setback home
the god damn phone ringing with middle age women
trying to sell me a collection of shit
I don't need, for a discount
and I only have ten minutes
to make up my mind
and all I want is my rocks and vodka
A luxury
finally
Nirvana and sleep
my comforter smells like
pee and at this point I don't give a fuck
it is the only place I don't have
to think
about being human
*"GOOD MORNING TORONTO! IT'S A GLORIOUS MORNING
FOR YOUR DRIVE IN!"*

A minor difficult called....

~ *Mauro*

Across the street
exactly next to the Roman Catholic Church
there lived Mauro
and his mama
in a chamomile life
sweet
he bade me a good day
every day
as he passed my door
toward work
my smile
bigger than his lips

Mauro loved me
tho, we never met bodies

There was one occasion only
when he stopped to bring me a gift

I cannot quite get this out of my mind
red Shiny Shoes with heels from hell
taller than him

An inscription under the soles spoke
puttana
and I could not help to think
'yes, please'

~ Soar

       I soar
through the grounds of this breaking heart
where every toe crunched on my bones tears your insidious name
glued toward me
yet
       i soar
for the child born to be raped by a solider as they stand on the
highway
of heroes
praising the real criminals
yet
       i soar
for the young girl who is not called to
eat at the dinner table
to feast alone on a dirty stairwell
one pea drop remains green
cold
yet
       I soar
for the father who drops his arms in
defect for the son who snorts his last stroke of cocaine
as his cardio arrests his soul and dies
       I soar
for the indifference of those who can complete a fucking
sentence without using
me
myself
and
       I
            Soar   Please Rise

~ Suitcases

he told me before he left this earth,
whilst you live
you will be penniless
but the suitcase you keep by the door will be full
of memories of *when*

the gale blows harder in the eve now
i pay more attention to them
messages coming through
spirits of awakening
there once was a time of sleep
i longed for it hourly
a bed made of cotton sheets
oh to dream those precious dreams
but without him dreams are old
of meaningless illusions
of emptiness within
and while the suitcase rests
against my waiting door
it does not quite have the effect
of rushing winds

Liberta

On the outskirts of every agony sits some observant
fellow who points.

~ **Virginia Woolf**

~ Liberation

There is a liberation when you step away from the crowd
Transferring your mind in thinking you are one of those smooth
wooden canes
Gracelessness as your ankles drift by the gathering egos
People tend to shift their eyes toward you
Only for a moment

I want to be forgotten yet desired
As big as an ancient Maple tree
and as tyrannical as an echoing wind
Instantly here
then gone

I want you to feel the embarrassment of a dark skin
Ancestors on ships smelling of moldy cheese and rotten figs
young parents hold their parents
land of dreams
to turn hard work
bad health
addiction to reminiscences of the old country
Because then you would
understand the importance of my feeling
for liberation

~ *Homeward Bound*

a complicated sadness
that suffers because of others
and the sofa it rests on
has a massive crease in the seat
I have tried to paint the walls
a sunflower to brighten those days
but colours are not where words lay
and in the bed that should be golden
upon the pillows of my dreams
the rushing water that scares my wake state
drowns me in my sleep
the voices coffers to my thoughts
that close more each day
the uninviting and horrid memories
of rejection never stray
this is my sadness
although it is something I want not to own
my throat has closed
and time is lost
and my anger fuels in droves
convince yourselves you know me
and rest assured in your souls
that I am just a tapestry
of muse that never grows

~ Writer

You are non-conforming
and unconventional
God is a subject in white
sex is rubbish

metaphors are empty
the abstract thoughts
you don't write about
annoy the publishers

unmolested language
poetry that is larger than life
you tick away, naked and
intoxicated
with an opened view
from your flat
to the tracks where
the insignificant
wander around the clock
open to nothing but empty wallets

you talk too much
because the faces that are
listening have since died
mid sentence
but you write
because without it
you are nothing
and because of it
you are the world's eyes

I picked up
a deep dark wound
and I carried it with me
until I died

Just the Whore You Wanted ~

Be damned
Be shamed

For nothing good are you.
You are nothing but pure and undying evil.

Be thrown and cast out, wither away, so that others may stomp on your ashes. Come, hungry tigers to feast on your flesh so that you feel pain for you know no pain like the one you created in me.

Be gone into the brightest light
for a brief glimpse at what you will never see again
fire!

Oh muse, muse, how my fingers
bleed on this doomed and dreadful fortress he built for me

bleeding so like a dam broken from the wrath
of the hollow soul that devours my veins and feasts at my liver

Death cometh soon on this infamous night
where betrayal and corruption feed at my ever
so corroded despair

Lead me, oh holy Jesus,
to the damnation of this lustrous life

Forsake me for I am mad, so trapped within the core of my shell and beaten
with sunken words, that I may feel all the horror I have done to he I so
spoke words of love to. Take me beyond the crystal eyes that stare me blind
in the night and cast me away oh sweet Lord. Fire me up! Let me burn in
the shadows of hell. I am a traitor that breathes nothingness and nonsense
into my lover's stomach. Blaming my madness is not what I will do now!

I blame nothing on no one but my condemned spirit
a soul that has become reckless in my consequence of life.
Consoling the one I love now is no use to what I have done.
This is not my world any longer. I live my life through fear.

Let me suffer my storm.

Oh muse, sorrowful muse, nervous and straying, muse.

Drifting in the prison of my mind that manifests

all the infuriating thoughts that I have made.

Oh sweet heavenly Father take me now

if for nothing else to make me suffer, truly suffer, the heat, the coals I

placed under my lover's feet.

Abuse this naked being that stands before you.

Head hung low

Begging to be torn

to shreds by savage mutants in your keep

Pity me not brave being

swallow me now, pity me not and

move my soul away from me so that I may not have

this deadly life

~ Appreciation

Poetry heals the wounds inflicted by reason.

~Novalis

Jennie Clarke holds a degree in Commonwealth Literature from York University and pursued a career in library science. An accomplished writer, her passion for books in all genres is now her labour of love. Inspired by great poets such as William Blake, Virginia Woolf and Charles Bukowski, Jennie began writing about the darker side of life. By day, Jennie moves her passion of words by working as a Librarian: by night, she is a muse.

Poetry can be interpreted in infinite ways, which is why she feels that poetry is the most beautiful language alive. Jennie does not write to please the masses, rather she represents the voice of many who are silent in this world.

This is her third book of poetry. Her first book in 1998, *Muse: a collection of poetry* saw huge universal success. Jennie was also the collaborative editor of *Held*, an anthology she compiled with fellow writers and poets. As a freelance writer, having published for newspapers, journals and anthologies, Jennie is currently working on *Jackets of House Arrest*, a collection of short stories.

Made in the USA
Charleston, SC
13 October 2016